The Friendship Book

Ariele M. Huff & Lotta Folks

ISBN: 1979900353
ISBN-13: 978-1979900355

Dear Reader: A book about friends by some of my friends. The topic has always interested me. I'd be delighted to hear your take on friendship or one friend. It may be used in the website segment I host (Sharing Stories) through *Northwest Prime Time* or might be added to this eBook or paperback. With love, Ariele M. Huff

ACKNOWLEDGMENTS

When I began asking for pieces about friendship, including specific friends, I had no idea how many people would want to participate. I did apply usual rules about only using quality work (though I do edit EVERYONE). I'm acknowledging both the people whose work has been chosen and those who did not make that cut. Your ideas have all helped me shape the book as well as my ever-evolving definition of what it is to be a friend and to have friends. Thank you, dear ones, for your thoughts and feelings on the subject. I'll never think of friendship or friends quite as I did before this project. I hope The Friendship Book brings similar aha moments to readers. (Title page photo: Ariele & dear friend, Norlisa Keffer.)

WHAT IS A FRIEND?

A friend is someone you can depend on. Someone who will be there when needed. One who seems to recognize your need. Offers to drive you to the dentist or doctor appointment, one like my neighbor who helps me with my yard work. Someone who is pleasant to be around, spend the day with—enjoying a bowl of clam chowder, sitting by the water watching the boats go by, just enough time to go to the movie we had planned to see.

Another friend likes to check on me once a week to see if I'm all right. She too likes to help in the yard and after that, munches on cheese and crackers in my back yard.

Another friend got me to the hospital and helped me while I went through total knee surgery two times, later, took me for x-rays when my new knee was injured.

I can count my close friends, who are near to my heart, on five fingers of one hand. Don Sivertsen's book Laughs, Luck & Life https://www.amazon.com/dp/B01IFN4DD8

Don with a couple of writing class friends (Connie Campbell and Melba Walton)

A LETTER A DAY

One recent afternoon, I suddenly got an idea about how to chase away the blues in a new way. What if I wrote a letter to one of my best friends every day for 30 days?

Despite my daily regimen of good self-care, I knew something was missing. I hadn't treated myself to any "Marla time" in months. "Marla time" is when I sit down and write my heart out to Marla Greenway, a dear woman friend and treasured pen pal.

When I write to Marla, I sometimes whip out ten or fifteen handwritten pages at a time. Even then, the only reason I stop is because I get hungry or tired. Marla devours every word of my letters with gusto. And when she gets to the end, she wants more. How cool is that?

It heals me to write to Marla because it's the closest thing I've ever experienced to writing to myself. She's not just "anyone else," either. She's someone who truly listens, and she listens with love.

I remember taking another longtime friend, Joe Rahn, to my parents' house for dinner in 1984, when I was 30. My older brother was also there. Afterward in the car, Joe asked if I had noticed that my parents didn't listen to me when I spoke. He said, "When you talk, everyone just ignores you and keeps talking. But when your brother speaks, your parents put down their forks and listen."

I was stunned, not only because Joe was right, but also because I'd never noticed it before. What he described was simply "normal" family behavior for me.

Obviously, it's disheartening when people who love you aren't interested in what you have to say. Because of this early conditioning, I still struggle sometimes to believe that Marla and others who love me are genuinely interested in me.

Writing to Marla for thirty days was so healing that I decided to keep going. And yes, I write to Marla by hand—three pages minimum, just like Julia Cameron's morning pages. But I do my "Marla pages" any time of day.

There is something magical about writing by hand. It slows me down and grounds me. It connects me more strongly to the physical world. Plus, I love knowing that the paper I'm holding in my hands will soon be held by the hands of a woman I dearly love.

Sometimes I still get blue, but writing about it to my friend Marla changes everything. Marla, my compassionate witness, changes everything—her friendship changes everything.

Cat Saunders, Ph.D. Counseling and Consultation, Author, *Dr. Cat's Helping Handbook: A Compassionate Guide for Being Human* www.drcat.org (photo) Cat Saunders (left) and Marla Greenway

THE SEASONS OF OUR FRIENDSHIP

Blue dragonflies flit about in front of us. The brown dried leaves crunch under our feet. An orange butterfly dances about the fragrant Rosa rugosas. It is summer, one of the many seasons of my 20-year friendship with Cara.

We met at the gym when Cara walked up and started chatting with me. The gym closed in an economic downturn, but we remained friends and started walking together. Eventually we joined another gym, but continued our twice-weekly walks.

We share our joys, our sorrows, our hopes and our dreams. There was my dad's sudden death, the weddings of her two sons, my mom's 80th birthday. If it has been a bad day, we can vent and laugh afterwards. I share many of the intimate details of my life and know that Cara can be trusted to keep my secrets.

As we walk along, Cara tells me that she and her husband hope to retire in the next three years and move closer to her grandchildren. I feel sad, but at the same time, I feel very blessed and lucky to have found this truly special friend in my lifetime. We walk along knowing that fall will be approaching soon with its brilliantly colored red, yellow, and orange leaves swirling in the wind. Another one of the many seasons of our friendship.

Carol R. Newman (Photo of Cara, left, and Carol)

AN ASPECT OF FRIENDSHIP

One thing I appreciate about living in the same space as with family is the continuity of conversation. That conversation which can be continually recalled without constraint of time and space. A commonality that confirms our humanity...ourselves as belonging. Melba Walton

FRIENDSHIP

I am trying to learn how to be a friend--and how to think about friends. I have come to the conclusion that I need to keep working to learn to cherish and challenge myself and at the same time keep working to cherish each unique person who is in my life. I can offer myself as a witness--and cheering section if they want to challenge themselves. Love from Mary Eva Love, Bright Morning Star

FRIENDSHIP

One time I was talking with my friend, Françoise, about what friends were, how to say it. The way she verbalized it was so different from mine that I don't remember it. I just remember being amazed that she saw it from such a different aspect. I never would have thought of looking at things that way yet I absolutely agreed with everything she said. The words she chose were perfect—well-crafted and thoroughly thought through. The feeling of that in-depth expression of sentiment lingers to this day, a solid, true connection to the core of my being. Looking back, maybe she was a philosopher in everyday garb, a deep thinker. To me, the French have a way of looking at life from a different side that expands, adds fullness to my own view. And I like that. C'est la vie.

Another deep and lasting impact came from the divorce of two friends. The words I used at the time were "I can't take sides." I felt torn in two. One was a long time, true friend from the days of our youth. The other was a living expression of my people's whole way of life, the struggles, sorrows, eked out joys, survival. I couldn't be against myself. Yet my dear, longtime friend had stood beside me through my own hard times with breakups, divorce, widowhood, staying true to clarity and caring. Staunch, loyal, never wavering, holding me up when I couldn't go it alone. To this day, we are still friends but the quality of the goodness was wounded, changed forever by those words. Sadness, sorrow, regret at the way life worked out may help friendship move on. But if the support isn't there when you go to lean on it, there's no way to undo the fall. Frieda Kirk

A HASTY EFFORT TO JOIN IN THE FUN

Friends come in all shapes and styles. Although the length of time spent together matters, finding common ground in our life stories and our inner joys and struggles matters far more. I lost track of my best friend in high school after our first year of college; 38 years later we took up again at our 40th reunion. Friends do that: pick right up where they left off. Friendships evoke positive memories even though we don't see each other. Shari playing her viola, Kay getting on my motorcycle for a picture, come to mind. Sharing my stories with friends by writing, reading, and listening enlarged my world view, helped me experience common ground and different perspectives. It seems to me the most important aspect of friendship is sharing, and I'm old fashioned enough to value face time over Facebook.

Paul Stocklin (Photo Paul and Kay Chelemedos on his motorcycle)

FRIENDSHIP

Friendship is an interesting subject. What is it that makes a person "click" with you—while another leaves you cold?

As an only child, with scattered relatives, my friends mean a great deal to me. I really don't know how I would have managed after my son's death without my dear and wonderful friend Valerie.

But I was born into friendship with Alma! Our mothers met and became friends in the maternity ward. Alma and I were born within 24 hours of each other. We kept in touch until she died about three years ago.

In my mid-teens, I became friends with Virginia, who lived in my neighborhood for a year. She is gone, too.

In high school, I palled around with Rosalind, who was as short as I was tall—so they called us "Mutt and Jeff" after a cartoon of the day. Peter and I visited Roz (now a widow) when back East last June.

Although I cannot for the life of me remember how I met Helen Cosgrove in NYC (1940), we visited and kept in touch. Helen died about 30 years ago of cancer.

Ruth and I met through friends in the 40s—and again, we hit it off and still visit and call each other, though she now lives in Southern California and I live in Seattle. We know some of the same people back home. What memories this brings! Kay Chelemedos

FRIENDSHIP

The dictionary words about friendship that I like are rapport, unity, attachment, bond, warmth, closeness, mutually sustaining. A friend is simply defined as a person whom one likes, knows, and trusts. So easy to like and know. Trust is tricky and long-term friendships often cross through tough times, the unexpected or difficult things to accept. Being accepted despite flaws or mistakes seems as close to a universal desire from friendship as I can detect.

My opinion is that we all have varied definitions of what makes a friend, depending on what we want or need in another person. I know I tolerate missing qualities in friendships if there's enough of any of the things I like to balance out the relationship.

Loyalty is the hardest for me to do without, though some people are tough to give up in spite of that lack. But I certainly am willing to be charmed by the amusing, entertained by the talented, and impressed by the clever. Humbleness and kindness really attract me. Frequently, I'm willing to hope for a deeper friendship based on those lures.

A friendship may lapse or be outgrown. Someone said early friendships drop away like milk teeth. But, friendships that serve a purpose, for a period of time, are valid as well as those that last, I think.

People who last as my friends are those who are as comfortable as I am with ebb and flow, who don't fence me in or place exacting rules on me. On my side, I'm willing to extend the same latitudes. I believe I am flexible, loyal, and forgiving. Those are traits I find in people who remain in relationships with me over longer periods of time. Ariele M. Huff

FRIENDSHIP

My cheeks always hurt after talking to Diana on the good old land line. We're both seventy-one years old, still laughing at the silliest things. I was groaning about not being able to slam-down the cordless phone if I got mad at an obnoxious caller. In an unplanned duet, we both announced, "Don't even ask about my smartphone!" We're a long way from current life in our time capsule of memories: listening in on party lines, Superman stripping in a five-cent payphone booth, or calling KJR radio station to "NAME IT AND CLAIM IT" winning the latest 45 rpm. We've been friends since we were three years old, growing up together. Dialing for dollars has stopped trying to find us.

Our mothers and fathers were best friends. I've always been taller than Diana, and a year ahead of her in school. I was born in December. She was born in March. The age cutoff date for grade school students, around Halloween in October. My parents felt I should skip kindergarten and take my long legs into the first grade. I always thought I was nine months older than Diana. For some reason, at forty, a light bulb came on in my head, causing me to clearly realize I was three months older, December to March, not March to December. I was never accused of being a math-wiz. When I told Diana my revelation, we laughed, then she admitted always thinking I was nine months older too. I continue to tease her, "I'm younger than we thought, but, still older, and 'with age comes wisdom.'"

We were five years old when the pool instructor at the Ellensburg "Y" showed us how to blow bubbles, keep our eyes open in the water, and grip our ankles, learning the turtle-float. We were challenged to hold the edge of the pool and kick like tadpoles, float like guppies, stroke in a school of minnows, and progress up the fish-ladder—turning into swimmers.

We heard the call of the wild, joining Bluebirds when we were six-years-old. Our group of screaming girls met at a leader's home to make arts and crafts, earning beads and patches to decorate blue vests. Diana was great at gluing popsicle sticks together and creating little houses, boxes, and frames. I wanted to be outside, climbing trees—a Bluebird hidden in leafy branches.

We were seven years old the first time we went to Campfire Girls Camp Illahee, near Cle Elum, for ten days. Home permanent curls for a fashionably carefree head of hair, sleeping bags, and an official list of necessities packed by our moms. Away from home, a cabin with outdoor plumbing, adventurous hiking, and group activities all day long – it was easy to learn important names. The cook was called "Cookie," the nurse "Nursie," but Diana was still Diana. Our counselor told her, "Diana was the goddess of the moon." Diana informed her, "I want to be an Indian Princess."

As we ate breakfast, lunch, and dinner at long tables, the noisy sounds of chewing, clanking silverware, and shouting voices were signs the girls felt camp comfortable. Heaven help you if a counselor caught your elbows resting on the table. Chanting began, "April, April, young and able, get your elbows off the table." The rhythm grew, over and over, until everyone joined a deafening chorus aimed at a red-faced Bluebird, hands clutching elbows. Not exactly an Emily Post moment in manners, but memorable.

One morning, all the Bluebirds gathered around a huge campfire. Counselors ordered everyone to pair up in teams of two. Diana and I stuck together. Passing frying pans to each team, they explained we were in a race to see who could fix the quickest breakfast—no time to dawdle. A counselor stood by the fire, describing how to cook bacon, toast, and eggs.

I got the bright idea, if we cooked eggs first, we would be the fastest cooks. When I explained my egg-theory to Diana, we agreed it would be a good shortcut. I cracked eggs into the pan, cooking up a surprising gloppy-eggy mess. Scraping the unrecognizable blob onto our plates, I put bacon in the pan, and heard a counselor mumbling, "What have you done?"

I quietly said, "I thought if we cooked the eggs first, we'd be the best cooks."

She loudly informed me, "You were wrong and should have listened to the instructions." She walked away, growling like a mad bear.

I looked down at the hissing bacon, hoping to hide tears swelling in my eyes. Diana touched my shoulder, "It's o.k., April. I'm sure it will still taste good." She was right. It did taste good, didn't look good, but had a smoky campfire flavor, sprinkled with kind words from a true friend.

As our friendship grew, Diana had clear ways of letting her opinion be known. If I did something she didn't like, she wouldn't hesitate to ask, "Who do you think you are, The Queen of Sheba?" Her answer to the unanswerable was, "Well, a skunk doesn't smell its own smell!" Whatever that meant, it seemed to fit everything. If I really annoyed her, she'd yell, "You snot-locker," making me laugh at her frustration.

During our adult lives, we kept in touch, but busy times…and life…got in the way. We grew apart for a number of years. After I turned sixty, the phone rang and on the other end of the line, a soft voice asked, "Is this April Ryan?" "Yes," ready to hang-up if it was a sales call. The voice replied, "I'm Diana. Do you remember me?"

"For goodness sakes, we were raised like sisters, of course I remember you." Now we talk on the phone every week. One day, I told her how nice it is that we grew up together in the beginning of our lives, and now we're together at the end, completing a full circle. She informed me, "This isn't the end, you snot-locker."

How do you describe a special friendship throughout a lifetime? She has become a true sister, part of my heart. Sometimes, possibly during a full moon, she is sister of The Queen of Sheba.

April Ryan April's pieces fill Sharing Stories at https://www.northwestprimetime.com LOCAL page, and she has pieces in *Holiday Sampler, Guilty Pleasures, Fifty Shades of Graying,* and *Housekeeping.* Photo (April & Diana)

THE FRIENDLY MENAGERIE (a poem)

Friends are like bears—who provide hugs when warmth, strength and love are needed.

Friends are like eagles—who fly in and out of your life providing you with support and help at the most appropriate times.

Friends are like tigers—who defend you against your enemies.

Friends are like giraffes—who give you advice from their point of view.

Friends are like kangaroos—who hop right in and help you in time of need.

Friends are like elephants—who have ears and hearts large enough to listen to our endless conversations.

Friends are like horses—who carry you on your life travels wherever your journeys take you.

Friends are like turtles—who, no matter how old or slow you become, are right there beside you.

I dare say, I live in a zoo where all my friends are caged in my heart.

Dedicated to all my friends, near and far, who have shared my journey for the last 75 years, a grateful friend, Tish Gregory.

VISITING FRIENDS

When they arrive, they come in like a Fighter Squadron—wings flashing, darting, dodging and in for a pinpoint landing. They have a strut and a hop; their glistening feathers shine as they have their free breakfast. A table spread on the front lawns. They leave many unanswered questions after they fly off.

For example: Who taught them that onions and green peppers are bad for their digestive systems? They can separate out what is good for them. How do they know? While they are eating breakfast, the Great White Knights (sea gulls) arrive. There is sizeable pushing, squaring, and duding over a choice piece. When the table is cleared, they regroup and are gone for the day.

My bushy tailed friend will let me know he has arrived by running up and down the tree outside my window until I see him. When I open the front door, he is watching—brown eyes sparkle to see which way I'll throw his treat. What a lovely friend, so sleek, bushy tail that never stops, able to climb up or head down quick as a wink.

What a pecking order: I have a wild black cat who lives under the shed in the backyard. He rules the entire group. When he shows up, they are gone. He can take his pick of whatever is being served. I love this cat. He is as wild as the wind. If I step out, he is gone. A flat out burst of fur in action, headed for his hole under the shed. We haven't seen a mouse since he arrived. Three years now. I'm sure happy he is a Tom, as one like this one is enough.

When we had geese in the back yard, the wild ducks would fly in for a free meal. One duck tried landing on the back fence. His feet were not designed to sit on a fence, but he tried real hard. I laughed so hard I cried.

I once bought a goat. Brought her home and put her in the backyard. At about two in the morning, my dog Shane wanted to check her out. The goat jumped seven feet straight up and landed on the wood pile. She took off through the neighbors' yards—me in hot pursuit, in and out of neighbors' yards too. It was a wonder I didn't get shot. Finally, I roped her and brought her home, put Shane in the house, and went to bed.

The next morning, I couldn't find her. While mowing the backyard, I heard her bleat. We had a tree climbing goat! She spent more time in the trees in the backyard than on the ground. Her time was short lived here. She caught me bending over, working on the lawn mower and butted my rear end with enough force to send me over the lawn mower. A lady from Snohomish picked her up that day.

Goodbye, Goat! Roger Wilson
Loving Life: A Roughneck's Guide to Having It All
http://www.amazon.com/dp/B00OEHXA3Y

FRIENDSHIP

A friend is a person who does not walk away when someone comes along they deem more important, they are always with you, be they near or far.
Connie Campbell

Connie and Ariele with Connie's *Church Cat* book.

THE IMPORTANCE OF FRIENDSHIPS

David Henry Thoreau once said friendship was "...one of life's great rewards."

I agree. Close friendships have been important to me all my life. They are relationships I enjoy and need. To form and maintain friendships requires the work of both people. I am very willing to be proactive in this work.

My longest -term friendships are from going through school in Bellevue. I grew up with these friends sharing maturing experiences. We played together, studied together and socialized together. Many of my friends have remained in Bellevue making it easier to continue these friendships. Some of my friends dating back to the third grade are Jeanne and Judd Haverfield, Geoff Clark, and Don Brockett. We all make new friends, but we can never replace the friends of our youth.

Kerri and I have many other long time friends. My buddies from our hike group and their spouses have been friends for 40-50 years. We socialize and go places together. Marlies and Dick VanCise have been friends nearly that long as has friends we met while living in Everett. Anna Karin Svenson we met when we moved to our Phantom Lake house in 1966.

Some of our closest friends are people who we have met through church. We share interests and enjoy the same activities. They were very supportive in my recent problems with MSA even to the extent of helping us move. One day fourteen of them were working on our move.

The downside of having longtime friends is that we are all getting old. We have lost some high school friends and several other friends have died. Many of our friends have illnesses, and we never know if we are going to see them again. The lesson is—do not procrastinate!

A unique and special friend is John Terrey. He was my high school English teacher 57 years ago. He went on to get his PhD and then become the executive director of Washington State community colleges. During his fifteen-year tenure he increased the number of community colleges from 18 to 36, so he has indirectly helped many students.

John and I have lunch two or three times each year. He tells me the story behind the story of what was happening while I was in high school. I was a good student, but John gave me my only B grade. I keep telling him it is never too late to correct a mistake. He better hurry, as he is 88 years old.

Now that we have moved into our Canterbury Shores condominium we are making more friends here. We enjoy having both long-term friends and new ones.

My closest friend in all aspects is my wife, Kerri. We have been friends for nearly 60 years!

Bill Lauman

BEST FRIEND

I caught the sweet voice of a lark
soaring above cheerful piano notes.
Peeking through a window, I saw curls;
my pounding heart told me we'd soon meet
We shared our deepest hopes and lofty dreams,
savoring each moment of friendship.
And you and I grew closer
till God Almighty united our hands.
We journeyed far to the islands
and grew to cherish a people not our own.
From our hearts and with a new tongue
we praised God and loved our fellow man.
Then, a surprise arrived, our family grew,
and then another, and another.
A princess and two warriors,
lives more precious to us than our own.
Life grew larger, fuller, busier;
yet through the fun, the tears, the pain,
you clung to me with arms of grace,
growing kinder and wiser each day.
The bustle of home has now stilled;
rooms are empty, closets are clean.
The fridge seems bare, the cupboards have less;
even the pooch is sleeping, counting her days
Yet our home is full, and I am content,
for you fill it with your light, your warmth.
And my affections remain steadfast,
my love, my delight, my best friend.
Gerrit Hansen

EVERYONE NEEDS A TRUE FRIEND

When my husband and I moved to Mountlake Terrace on February 22, 1961, I met my next-door neighbors, the O'Keefe family. The parents, Dennis and Cleo, had two children, Kathleen and Denny, and one on the way. We had Cindy and Linda and Jeff was due about the same time as their Ruthann. Other children were born later.

Cleo was such a gift to have as a neighbor. We shared the good times and the not so good times. After my husband left me with the three little ones, I often relied on Cleo for an ear to listen, good advice and just having someone who cared.

One year, after I married my second husband, we had twins, Timothy and Kimberly. My older children were then all in school. I was a stay-at-home mom since I could not earn enough to justify daycare. It was not easy to go anywhere with two babies. The old-fashioned twin strollers were side-by-side, so most stores didn't have wide enough aisles. I don't know how I would have survived that first winter without Cleo coming to visit with me.

Our children grew up together. We each had a large piece of land for them to run and play. My family had a playhouse. The children could go to either yard without asking, but they could not go to any other neighbors without first getting permission. Whenever one of the parents called children to come for a meal, they all had to go home to their own yards.

The O'Keefe's had similar rules and expectations in raising their children. Cleo was a good cook, and we all used many of her recipes. She was an excellent seamstress. When I took a beginner sewing class at Edmonds Community College, I went next door for her help with my sewing mistakes. She always had a solution. She even took a candle making class and shared how to do that with me. One year, I sold candles along with boxes of Christmas cards to make gift money for my children.

Cleo was a huge blessing in my life and helped me through the years of raising children. I wish all families could have such a good neighbor.
I hope I was a good friend to her too.
Joan Minnis

FRIENDS AND RELATIVES

I have been to Norway. I had a chance to visit relatives at the big homestead farm where my family's ancestors lived. Some are still living on the property. The log building is now in an outdoor museum, sixty miles away in Molde, Norway.

I was sitting in my backyard the other day, explaining about my trip to Norway and about Bjørnstjerne Bjørnson who wrote novels and the words to the Norwegian National Anthem. I learned from my third cousin who spoke fluent English why the log cabin, now an outdoor museum with other old buildings, brought people together—for all to see at Romsdal Museum in Molde.

I was told the author wrote a novel that high school students are required to read. Synnøve Solbakken, a story of the land, the house, and little Synnøve who grew up there…and the boy across the førd who admired Synnøve.

My Norwegian relatives encouraged me to read the book. I also read another—Glad Gut (means Happy Boy in English). I found the books at the Seattle library. They were tattered and torn. I made copies of the books, and I feel gratified to learn so much about my relatives who lived so many years ago. I'm still learning.

When I told my niece and her children about my trip, Dorothy (who is good on the internet) listened closely. She was so interested that she came up with something that surprised me. Yesterday, I went to a birthday party for my niece's husband Craig—just turned sixty. Everyone was smiling when I came in. Don, do you want to see a movie? (I knew they subscribed to Netflix, so this wasn't a complete surprise.) The movie is in black and white. It's a "Silent"—no talking, only Norwegian captions. People asked me,
"Can you read it?" Yes…enough that I can catch the meaning when I read.

Dorothy had found a silent movie called Synnöve Solbakken, directed in 1919, showing my family's house farm and the surrounding hillside. I was overwhelmed. It was four hours long. I watched for one and a half hours, then reception stopped. I don't know why.

Now, I know the story about people 200 years ago! A story of farming people, dressed in the garb of their era and place. I could not have been more pleased. I hadn't known the movie existed. How many people can watch a movie of their ancestors acted out? Like I could, with Synnöve Solbakken?

It's good to have so many relatives and friends. All this happened to me because I attended a Norwegian language class a year ago. The teacher encouraged us to contact and write to our relatives.

I found they were warm friends…here and in Norway.

This having real friends is real wealth!

Don Sivertsen *Laughs, Luck & Life from A to Z:*
https://www.amazon.com/dp/B011FN4DD8

SOMEHOW

It's midnight on a Monday, and I sit beside you in the darkness, smoothing your brow for what may be the last time. You draw slow breaths and sleep a restless sleep. A sleep interrupted by pain, or maybe dreams, or maybe the unknown questions of what tomorrow brings.

I can't imagine what sparks of thought or understanding move through your consciousness, just like I can't really know what you are going through. But what I do know...what I do know is that I don't want to see you in pain anymore. What I do know is I've done everything possible these last weeks to make you more comfortable, to make things more bearable. But I see your struggle and the frustration in your eyes, and I know our time is growing short.

Tears pool beneath my eyelids when I think about you leaving. I wonder whether you can see what lies ahead. A light at the end of a dark tunnel? A familiar face beckoning? Or maybe a green meadow beside a still pond where you can cool your tired feet. If only I could see it with you, to know all will be well.

I try to comfort myself with the memory of your old beauty and strength. Irrationally, I wish I could turn back the clock to yesterday—to sit beside you on the patio in the warm spring sun, watching mottled brown lizards skittering along the wall. Or hike the slopes of Stormy Mountain and rest at the summit, while rain clouds spill over the Cascade ridge tops. Such simple things.

But yesterday has passed. We'll never do those things together again, you and I. I know this...I do.... I know it the same way I know that when you fly free, I'll weep, wishing we had one more day. And that years from now, I'll still speak aloud to you even though you aren't there, your memory an ache in my heart. There is no replacement for you, my friend. And somehow, one of these days, I'll have to learn how to make peace with that.

Sandy D'Entremont

FRIENDS

This is not a day to write about friends. I am alone and the house is silent. I turned on the radio—King FM—for sound, but it is gloomy. I have exhausted my phoners. It is too early to call Joe in the nursing home. Joe was my student at West Seattle High School in 1946. I am the only person who calls him. His roommate is speechless and senseless. Poor Joe. He says the food is terrible. One day, he said lunch was Greaseball Soup in Thirty-Weight Oil.

It's just that today was a blue-gray day. Don't misunderstand me. I do have friends. Up to 2002, my sisters were my lifetime friends. Dorothy gave me flute lessons and kept me in knitted sweaters until a year before she died. Frances was my counselor and mentor until Alzheimer's took away all but the moment. My daughters have been staunch friends. My neighbors are supportive and friendly.

I shouldn't forget my kitty, Jelly Bean. She is a great friend. In her mind, I am a somewhat faulty person, here to do service for Jelly Bean. She sweetly forgives me for my shortcomings and daily gives me some quality time, with hugs and kisses. She rises to the occasion when I need help. She makes a great fuss and tries to do something when I fall down. She has one people word, "Grandma"—believe me she does, but won't let anyone else hear her. She stands between me and unappealing strangers. She is a true friend according to her lights.

I think friendship is a sometimes thing, a treasure when it happens, and…I should write this again tomorrow!

Pat Sweazey

A FRIEND IS ONE

who listens when

you're feeling low,

and understands;

and by your side

in troubled times,

extends a hand.

who shares with you

when there is joy

that overflows,

and cares about

the secret you

that no one knows.

You are that friend.

Martha Lindquist

THE MEANING OF FRIENDSHIP

The friends that I have seem to fall into groups or "families." There are the friends I have in my Water Aerobics class. When someone in the group gets sick or has an operation, we all care enough to send a card or call to find out how they're doing. The same is true of my Fine Arts Study Club and my string quartets. No matter what the occasion, we bolster each other with cheery wishes and sharing of news, whether good or bad.

My church friends are also very special people. They really care when you're having a bad day or need extra attention or have good news to share. The friends in my writing class are privy to all my stories, both good and bad. Their support and encouragement are very confidence inspiring.
After my recent operation (laporoscopic kidney removal), many people were helpful, sending us food and cards and being generally good friends.
I think I'm a good friend to my children and grandchildren. Right now, Dan and I drive to South Seattle twice weekly to our grandson, Nate's pre-school to pick him up after school and take him to our daughter's H.S. Library in Edmonds, a total of 16 miles. We also are giving our youngest son, Bret, board and room while he looks for housing that he can afford. During my recovery from surgery, Dan and Bret did all my kitchen chores, getting meals, washing dishes, etc. They wouldn't let me in the kitchen, so I was able to get well very quickly.

So, I guess my best friends are my family and my various "families" are truly my friends. And, in order to have friends, I must be a friend. Shari Peterson

Shari's beloved viola—friend of another kind!

MY VERY, VERY BEST LONGTIME FRIEND—EMMA WATCHIE

In third grade when my family moved to Seattle, I quickly made friends with Emma Watchie. There were only about 16 kids in our class, and the other four or five girls didn't interest us much. Emma lived pretty close to me, but other than that, I can't imagine what she saw in me.

Emma, or Butch, was the youngest of five kids and probably nine years younger than her nearest sibling, Rita, who was in HIGH SCHOOL. Marian was at the UW, a Kappa Kappa Gamma, beautiful, sophisticated, and totally unapproachable. There were two boys, really old, nearly finished with college. They had jobs, drove cars, and were known to jump or dive off the University Bridge for money. One of them had a large quarter collection which he kept in a tennis ball can; I remember that we sometimes helped ourselves. I was pretty scared of all of them. Emma's dad called her "Squirt" and everyone else called her "Butch." Her mom was not well, and, as far as I could tell, she played bridge every day. This family in no way resembled mine.

Butch didn't ride bikes, roller skate, or play outside really, and I didn't cook, do housework, or help out much at home. Seems like we had very little in common. As the years went by, we "hung out" a bit, as kids today would say. We liked to walk to the Broadway District or the University District and poke around in shops. These were all day excursions. We also snooped around under the University Bridge and the houseboat area down there. Eventually, that became a good place to smoke.

In the summer after seventh grade, Butch's Mom died. Butch grew up really fast after that. In our eighth-grade picture, I see she was almost a head taller than I was. She was developing a pretty little figure and wore fashionable clothes. Boys liked her and she liked them. I, on the other hand, was getting braces on my teeth, was super skinny, socially inept, and was still doing things like trying to fly off the garage roof with an umbrella. Nevertheless, the friendship endured.

When we got to high school her dad drove us to school every day, and we walked home together every afternoon. We started smoking at about 16, using our bus money for cigarettes (they cost 23 cents per pack). We walked most of the way on Interlaken Boulevard; an area much like a park, where nobody could see us. Nobody would have seen us being murdered or kidnapped either, but luckily that didn't happen. (I wouldn't walk around in there today.)

I suppose most long-term friendships ebb and flow like the tides—ours certainly did. We were always in touch, but didn't always spend time together. In high school, we were in different crowds, then jobs, boyfriends, husbands, and children. And, we both moved away from Seattle for a time. Many years went by before we re-connected in 1970 when I moved back and found myself living close to her neighborhood. Eventually, we were both divorced, and we began spending time together again and getting reacquainted. Over the years, we enjoyed many good times and cemented a friendship of more than 60 years. We loved to hash over the past and laugh and cry and reiterate the loving feelings we had for one another.

Sadly, Emma died about eight years ago in Palm Desert, California. I was able to attend her funeral and meet her golfing buddies down there at their winter getaway. I felt fortunate to be there for her husband, whom I really like, and for her step-brother a Catholic priest, also a good friend, who had the honor of officiating at her funeral service. I think of her often and wish she was still here. I always think of her on June 1st, her birthday. We never failed to connect on birthdays.

Thinking about Butch today, I remember how much she hated the name "Emma." It seems like everybody hated that name. So, time went by and the name Butch took on some other meanings and now many hate that name while Emma is popular. Who knew? Lois Caslin

Emma (Butch) Watchie grabbing a smoke at around 16.

MY FRIEND FOR BETTER OR WORSE

I'm blessed with such a wonderful husband, family, and friends. With that being said, I would like to tell you about one particular friend I've had for as long as I can remember. We have shared many good and bad times together. She has taken care of me with words of encouragement and, at times, told me what a damn fool I am. However, she has definitely led me down the wrong path once or twice too, though she did help me climb that long steep hill called the teenage years, also helping me put on the brakes going down the other side of that hill—called MIDDLE age… especially when I notice how funny it is that the person in my mirror looks so much like my mother…more and more every day.

Each day, my friend and I talk and say, "Ok, Kid, it's another day. Let's make it better then yesterday. I'm relying on you."

Mary Boley

I LIKED TOM

For a few years of my life he was my best friend. We parted ways, but I never had bad feelings about him. I will always remember him with a glow. But not all readers will like Tom. Those driven to amount to something will find him unworthy. Tom was the antithesis of driven. He let life drive him, but not helplessly. He didn't float the river of time like a leaf subject to the whims of fate. He floated downstream with conscious intent not to resist the current but to use timed strokes to avoid the major hazards. His last obstacle of cancer was an unavoidable dam, but he would have been fatalistic in accepting that.

People who liked Tom remember him fondly. He sticks out in afterthought, like when you discover a great truth and then realize that you really knew it all along. No one will remember Tom as mad, greedy, stingy, or mean. He was none of those things. He was warm, friendly and most of all funny. Funny "ha-ha" but also funny strange, but a strangeness that intrigued you rather than put you off.

Tom will be remembered for living life well. Not famously, but in a satisfying manner. Not satisfying to you, but satisfying to him, and he being satisfied somehow benefited you as well. Tom embodied the benefit of finding your own path. Not the path others want but the path you want. His example was there for all to see and has lasted even after he's gone.

Dick Gross

A FRIEND

Once, during the 47 years of friendship with Karyl, I heard her mention to others, "Helga would give you her shirt if you needed it."

Recently, during the scattering of her ashes near her favorite trail, I wore her hiking shirt. So many memories are woven into it—from wondrous rests on top of steep mountain peaks to scary moments when we pulled our kayaks into a safe Pacific cove before the storm.

Besides numerous strenuous climbs and hikes, we enjoyed many non-guided adventures together, in Southeast Asia, the Caribbean, or South America and Alaska's arctic region—totally relying on each other.

We shared awesome moments: looking underwater at myriads of colorful fish in the Andaman sea, enjoying the view of the Andes from the top of Machu Pichu, or spending hours under an overhanging rock in a Patagonian rainstorm, where it was Karyl who shared her raincoat with me.

A good friend gives up her own desires to help and love, or just to be there.

Helga Byhre Read Helga's exciting book *Views from the Hill* at lulu.com
Photo of Helga and Karyl on Snowking Mountain in the North Cascades

MY FRIEND, THE FISHERMAN

When the sun's shining bright
on a warm summer morn,
and the robin's sweet song
makes you glad you were born.
And you can't see a cloud
in the clear sky of blue,
then my friend, the fisherman
knows what to do.
He tells all his problems.
They'll just have to wait
and he picks up his hooks
and his tackle and bait.
Then he gets in his car
and with no backward look
he heads for the quiet
of his favorite brook.
Then settling down
in the shade of a tree
and listening to
the soft drone of a bee,
not turning his thoughts
to a worry or care,
he refreshes his mind
by the peacefulness there.
So, while all the rest
of the world rushes on,
not stopping to rest
till their whole life is gone.
Then my friend the fisherman
seems wise to me
cause he can find peace
in the shade of a tree.
Nancy Moyer

Nancy L. Moyer and her husband Donn J. have created an exciting book of landslides, earthquakes, fires, and other Washington State disasters. Find it at: https://www.amazon.com/dp/B01NAGFXG4.

MY FIRST BOY FRIEND

When I was five, I had a boyfriend who lived across the street from us. He was a year older than me, and his mother was my second-grade teacher and his father my principal in grade school. Johnny used to come over, and we would lie on the parlor floor and look at pictures in the encyclopedia and maybe he read—I don't remember. In the summertime, I went to his place, and we looked at comic books under the willow tree whose branches went to the ground. It was like our secret hide-a-way. One game I remember us playing at my home: We sat on the floor and rolled a ball to each other. If we did not catch it, we had to move to where the ball landed, even if it was in another room. We were all over the place when the ball bounced off something to send it to a hidden corner. I often wonder where Johnny is. He was my first boyfriend, at age five. Pat Beaudry

SPECIAL GIFT OF FRIENDSHIP

My husband, Bob Minnis, was critically ill in the hospital for several days. We knew he had cancer for one month. Bob had been planning to retire in six months when he turned 65. We had discussed making funeral arrangements when he retired. However, Bob died on April 30, 1993 about 9 am. There hadn't been time to make many decisions that I now had to make alone.

My daughters, Kimberly and Linda, helped me pick out a burial place and make all the preparations for a service. It took all day. We arrived home at about 6 pm, totally exhausted with no energy left to cook dinner. We'd spent so much time at the hospital, there wasn't much food in the refrigerator. We were all hungry, but we just sat at the table wondering what we should do about dinner.

We heard someone drive in. It was Stan Krahn, bringing dinner for us. Jeanne had made a delicious stew, salad, and bread. Everything was ready to eat. It was manna from heaven for us that day. This is only one of the fond memories of the wonderful friends Stan and Jeanne were through the years. Joan Minnis

THREE MUSKETEERS

Several times in my life, I've been part of a set of three Musketeers...three friends who balance each other, have a lot of fun, and enjoy the luxury of a spare friend when the other friend isn't available.

In my neighborhood, Sandy, Diane, and I were my first three-girl configuration. Diane and I were both oldest sisters, and Sandy was her family's only girl. Looking back, we were quite a powerful group—younger siblings to direct in our plans and games. We competed to be the main girl a few times, but mostly had fun.

In junior high school, I had a tight best friendship with Jeannette. No extra friends needed.

In high school, my new threesome pals were Roberta and Colleen. With more independence (Colleen drove and had a car), we had great fun and planned an overzealous trip to Lake Crescent that was squashed by worried parents. Lots of laughter in this group.

As a young mother, I had Nancy and Grace in my tight group, but Peggy who worked and Patrice who joined later were often part of our social gab and kid surveillance group. (We all lived in the same neighborhood with babies, then toddlers, then preschoolers.) Our relationships had a lot to do with analyzing parenting and marriage with some feminism, politics, and other brainy topics to give us some moments of adult focus. Nancy was oldest by ten years and had the most children so she was the undisputed Queen of the neighborhood. When she moved her gang to Hawaii (where she'd lived as a child), the group became less cohesive.

My most recent Musketeer alignment was with Connie (see earlier photo) and Judy. They both took my Greenwood Senior Center class and the three of us often went out together.

Dear Reader: As I write this, two of my closest friends, Connie and Melba, have life threatening problems. The joys of friendship are worth it, in spite of the pain of potential loss. My loving thoughts, prayers, and hopes to them…and to all of you and your friends. Ariele M. Huff

ABOUT THE AUTHOR

Ariele M. Huff: Columnist and freelance writer since 1979, writing instructor and conference speaker since 1982, pre-publication book editor (including fiction and nonfiction like the *LA Times* Outstanding Travel Book of 2002 and for the re-write of *The Pea-Pod Kids Pop-Up Book*, a Christmas best seller in '86, and *Allah's Garden*, 2009), and editor for over a dozen magazines, journals, and newspapers since 1980. 2002-2007: Senior Editor of *American Road* magazine which rated Mr. Magazine's "Top 30." Columns Poetry Corner and Writing Corner appear in *Northwest Prime Time News*, articles and a blog appear on an e-zine—http://www.barefoot-running.us/ .

I have over 20 eBooks and paperbacks which are available on Amazon.com and Createspace. I have hosted and produced radio programs and served as Acquisitions Manager for a regional publisher. I've helped/am helping numerous people write their personal stories or stories of family members. I've edited and assisted with many novels and nonfiction books.

Website: http://arielewriter.myfreesites.net
Web-host: Sharing Stories at http://northwestprimetime.com/ Local section

My columns Writing Corner and Poetry Corner are in the print version of *NW Prime Time* which is free at libraries and senior centers in the Seattle area. I teach onsite writing classes in the Seattle area and online classes to people all over the world. Email me for a complete list of class titles or with any writing questions you have. ariele@comcast.net

Made in the USA
San Bernardino, CA
02 December 2017